MY Love STORY

GREGORY L. BYRD SR.

WestBow Press books may be ordered through booksellers or by contacting:

WestBow Press
A Division of Thomas Nelson & Zondervan
1663 Liberty Drive
Bloomington, IN 47403
www.westbowpress.com
844-714-3454

ISBN: 978-1-6642-4760-4 (sc)
ISBN: 978-1-6642-4761-1 (e)

Library of Congress Control Number: 2021921380

Print information available on the last page.

WestBow Press rev. date: 01/19/2022

WESTBOW
PRESS®
A DIVISION OF THOMAS NELSON
& ZONDERVAN

MY *Love* STORY

I would like to thank my Heavenly Father. For putting in my heart to become a writer. I would like to give praise for all that he's brought me through and he's helping me with.

Also, I want to thank my children, who inspired me to seriously give thoughts to writing This best seller. But my wife has been my biggest fan and,my biggest critic. And most of all, she's the reason that this is all possible. I would like to thank her. I thank all who have inspired me.

Contents

Preface

Where do I start?
Well, let me start by saying that my name is Gregory L. Byrd Sr.

I enjoy being a father and husband as well as being a help to others. I'm the father of many kings and queens. I was born and raised in the great state of Missouri. I have lived in the Midwest most of my life. Just to name a few states I have lived in, they are Missouri, Indiana, Illinois, Michigan, and Wisconsin. I am the eldest of four children. How did I realize I wanted to become an author? Well, it was not until I took a literature class in college. I had to write an essay of 1,500 words or less, and the teacher and the others who looked over it liked it and gave me first place. It has been four years that I have been trying to write this book. Since I have been with this publishing company, I think it has really taken off. I plan to make it a best seller. It would give me immense pleasure if you will read it.

Chapter 1
The First Meeting

This is a story that has the right mixture of romance, adventure, and excitement. It started in the summer of 1977, which was the season to remember. The weather was great, the sun was shining, there were lots of laughs, the smell of cut grass was good, and it felt great to be on summer vacation. As I walked around town and met new people, it hit me that I did not have what they had: a girlfriend. I had just moved to Kalamazoo, Michigan, and I did not know anyone, but there was my sister. She knew a lot of girls from high school.

As the days went on, I met some friends of my sister, but they were not for me. One day, I picked up my sister's yearbook and started seeing faces she had never told me about. There was one person I really wanted to meet. But I couldn't let my sister know that I had been pillaging through her things. I finally convinced my sister to open her yearbook to see Joyce's picture again. After telling my sister that I wanted to meet her, I told her that if she could arrange it for me, I would be in her debt forever.

My sister made the call that would change my life forever.

I got to talk with Joyce, and it was very pleasant. As we talked, I was building up nerve to ask her out on a date. Eventually, she said yes, but where would I take Joyce? Wow! I had no funds; therefore, I had to ask my father, which I dreaded to do. But to my surprise, he gave me some money and said, "Have a good time." This date was the start of our relationship.

We would communicate by phone and occasional walks through town. We grew closer and closer, and our feelings for each other started to change. I could not stop thinking about her all day every day. And then one day, my aunt asked us to babysit her children while she ran to the mall. It was that day I found out what is meant by your "first love." It was such an experience that we both were overcome with passion. The thought of us not getting together again was unheard of. Yes, we took that plunge: the love plunge.

After that, we were inseparable.

Chapter 2
The Change

———— ♡ ————

Day in and day out, we were together no matter what, and we went everywhere together. And yes, we walked every step of the way hand in hand. It was truly our beginning of a great summer.

But the weeks rolled into months, and Joyce started to change. I mean her mood, shape, and even her waist started to spread. And Joyce's stomach got harder. She was always hungry, and she slept more than ever now. Why was she changing?

I noticed a change within myself as well. I began eating weird things, such as tuna fish on pizza, pickles, and ice cream just to name a few. Then my sleeping pattern changed, and I began to sleep a lot. I did not know what to think or to do about my present illness.

Then our families started to ask a lot of questions and to volunteer their theory about what could be wrong. No one actually seemed to say the things we thought they were going to say. Consequently, we would have to solve this mystery on our own.

The news we were about to receive would not be what typical, ordinary teens (fifteen years old) would expect. After all, we were about to find out something that would change our lives forever.

We were told to visit a Planned Parenthood office, where we spoke with a counselor for help. She asked, "What are your plans for the future, and did you plan on starting a family right now? And how are you going to take care of a child?"

We both froze, and our hearts sank.

Chapter 3
The News

That was only the beginning of our problems; our parents were going to hit the roof when they found out about this. This news from us would only have our parents thinking back to their beginnings. Yes, our parents on both sides were young, inexperienced parents. None of them wanted the same fate for us. But hiding was not an option. We knew we had to tell them.

But my first thought was to be together one last time. And Joyce agreed. Little did we know it would really be our last time.

So I walked Joyce home first, and then I went home. Before I got within fifty feet of the house, I heard my father yelling at the top of his lungs on the phone—with Joyce's mother on the other end yelling as well.

I went into the house, and my dad asked if I had something to tell him. I said "yes". And then we sat down. Carefully, making sure I chose the right words, I said, "Joyce is pregnant, and may I finish school here in Kalamazoo?" I explained how I wanted to help with the baby. My father looked sternly at me while peering over the frame of his glasses. Then he said, to my surprise, "If I can talk your mother into agreeing to it, it would be fine."

Chapter 4

Mom's Approval

———— ♡ ————

Well, knowing my mom, it would be hard to get it past her. But then the really bad news came. Joyce's mother said we were done and we could not see each other ever again.

Our families assumed we would not be able to care for a baby and finish school. So they felt they were doing the right thing by separating us. I was sent to live with my uncle in Illinois. We were so brokenhearted that all we could do was cry and say goodbye. We had no clue that it would take until our twenty-first birthdays before we saw one another again. Yes! It took five long years before I saw her again.

It was a joyous sight to behold. I did not pressure her to be with me, but part of me wishes I had, because it would be another *thirty years* before I saw them again.

Chapter 5

The Reunion

The years went by so fast that I wondered how they were, including how my son looked and how she looked for that matter. But fate stepped in and dealt the hand we had to live with. That hurt for many years.

We both got married to other people and went on with our lives, not knowing when or if we would see each other ever again; it was not until 2011 that I got a phone call from my uncle, who was at the funeral of another family member. I asked him if he would mind giving my number to my sister, who could get it to Joyce. I was so happy that there might be a remote chance I would hear from her and see my son, who is now a grown man.

I missed all the important things like teaching him to ride a bike, toss a baseball, and throw a football, just to name a few. And then, the day after Christmas 2011, my phone rang. I didn't recognize the number. After pushing the talk button and saying hello, the voice on the other end asked, "Is this Gregg?" I asked, "Who's this?" and she said, "It's me, Joyce."

At that moment, my heart fell to the bottom of my feet. I said, "Prove it. Tell me something that only we would know."

The line was silent for all of five seconds, and then she told me what the answer was. Then I knew it was Joyce.

So I said, "How have you been, and how and where is our son?" "Fine," she said with a happy tone I had not heard for many years.

So we started to talk and reminisce about old times and wonder what could have been if we hadn't been separated. But that turned to sad topics so we changed to something more soothing.

Then we switched up to talk about the lives of the other children we had had and our marriages to others, but it quickly turned back on us.

In May 2012, we met in Kalamazoo, Michigan, and began our reconnection.

I would come every other weekend and volunteer with Joyce on several organizations. We were doing things we both enjoyed. As the months progressed, I did not want to be away from her anymore. I decided to leave Milwaukee, Wisconsin, and move here to Lansing, Michigan. We got married the day before the election, and our honeymoon was spent getting our President Obama reelected.

Each and every morning I look into my best friend's face, I feel as if we have been together all along.

Chapter 6

Christmas of 2020

———— ♡ ————

Christmas of 2020 Will be one to remember that's for sure it felt different to say the least, I mean the tree was up holiday music was playing my wife and children and myself we were all at home, I mean the previous years when we traveled to spend time with family and meet at moms to eat some of my favorite dishes, and have fun as I remember it, but the pandemic of 2020 didn't let that happen so much changed so fast and you had to rearrange things we took for granted like going out to eat shopping school going to worship service the way we traveled, but most of all we lost contact with the human race as we knew it I mean social distancing no large gatherings no contact at all.

But through it all we had to keep our sanity and stay focused on the task at hand.

Merry Christmas from The Byrd's

Chapter 7
New Year's 2020

———— ♡ ————

New Years Celebration 2020 came in just right for my family and I in church giving our thanks to the father above even though it was virtual it still felt great its a tradition we do every year but this time we were as all other parishioners were at home watching on tv, but also we're here to see another year and to be healthy and strong going into this new year is a blessing in itself we can only pray that 2021 will be a better year for all mankind this would be a year that would try us as a whole because the pandemic spares no one from its grip we, became closer in these unsure days and the only resolution is to stay alive. We are in very uncertain times not knowing what to expect from day to day, so I say stay in prayer and keep your dam mask on.

Happy New Years from the
Byrd's

Conclusion

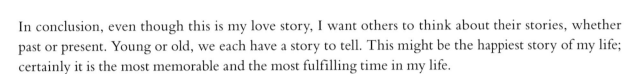

In conclusion, even though this is my love story, I want others to think about their stories, whether past or present. Young or old, we each have a story to tell. This might be the happiest story of my life; certainly it is the most memorable and the most fulfilling time in my life.

Love has no time limit. Love will find you when you least expect it. If love leaves you and returns, that was meant to be. It means everlasting love, so cherish it. Embrace it, for it is yours.

Printed in the United States
by Baker & Taylor Publisher Services